Memoirs of a Revolution Experience Through Poetry and Poems

LULU WESTBROOK GRIFFIN

Copyright © 2020 Lulu Westbrook Griffin
All rights reserved
First Edition

PAGE PUBLISHING, INC.
Conneaut Lake, PA

First originally published by Page Publishing 2020

ISBN 978-1-6624-0351-4 (pbk)
ISBN 978-1-6624-0353-8 (hc)
ISBN 978-1-6624-0352-1 (digital)

Printed in the United States of America

Contents

Introduction 7
Poetry 11

Family

Be 15
Father, Dedicated to You 16
Mama Dearest 17
Memory of a Loved One 18
Sister, Sister 19
Thoughts 20
Birthday Wish 21
Black Men: Make the Difference 22
Days of the Week 24
Breathless 25
The Earth 26
Free Spirit 27
If I Had My Way 28
I 29
Imagine 30
Shadow 31
Shakespeare 32
Smile 33
Springtime 34
Words 36

Spiritual

Angels 39
Easter 40
Faith 41
Hope 42
I'm Free 43
My Plea 44

Poem for a Small Child 46
Success 47
The Bible 48
My Soul 49
Down in My Soul 50
The Word 51

Love

Forever 55
Friend 56
Love Is 57
My Valentine 58
Struttin' Right Up 59

Black History

Africa 63
Discrimination Among Coloreds/Blacks
  (The Shade of Skin Tone) 64
Justice Let It Stand 65
Martin L. King and Elvis, the "King" of Rock 66
Once Upon a Time 67
Stand For What You Believe 68

Southern Memories

Move On 71
Po' Man 72

Childhood Memories

Barefoot 77
Children 78
My Town 79
Summertime 80
Leesburg Memories 81
Americus, Georgia in '63 82

Thirteen Is Ten plus Three 83
Misery 84
Memories of the Stockade 85
Traumatized 86
Black Night 87

Nightmares

After My Release from the Stockade 91
Reminiscence (Incarceration: 1965 Civil Rights) 92
Transition 94

Introduction

The early years of my life was racially divided because of the Jim Crow laws in my hometown of Americus, Georgia. During the fifties and sixties, tired "colored people" (at that era), the Southern terminology for black people / African American, were struggling to live in a dominated white society. The inferiority and subordination, one would say.

My reminiscence of my people's daily life was a very passive one. Economically, educationally (if there be a word), and socially speaking, or lack of these things, render them useless.

I was born pre-Civil Rights days into my psyche of blatant, obvious signs of segregation and words of segregation posted over public restrooms, water fountains, entrances at back doors of buildings with a white hand pointing that showed us where we were to enter.

The vestiges of colonial laws had all spurned from a slave mentality. I lived on a red dirt road in a noninsulated white clapboard house—a roof made of tin that was only noticeable when it rained or when one of my brothers was hitting the roof with rocks just to let us know that he was coming toward the yard. The rain sounded at times like beats to a drum, raindrops dancing to a musical beat. There were railroad tracks that separated the north side of town from the south side.

The older people had a lot of faith, love, and was very wise in knowledge of raising their children. Their wisdom came from praying and reading the Bible. They taught the children and grands good values, good morals, and used strap to chastise them was the way of life. It is very true that it takes a village to raise a child. The whole neighborhood of families looked out for others' children. Grandparents, uncles, aunts, cousins, and friends were always nearby. That was the love our people had for all people.

The disrespect came from white supremacy groups and separatists toward the poor and downtrodden. The colored people (so we were called) were condemned for the color of their skin tone.

They were humble people because of the condemnation upon them. I remember reports of news over the radio about violent beatings, harmful acts, senseless harassment, and crime toward my ancestors, other people of color, and elderly people all the time. Violence was always perpetrated on us citizen in my hometown. They were humble people. There were good days as well. My family had gatherings, such as birthdays, Easter Sundays, holidays, and Christmas with all-day church services. I had many chores also to do. Growing up in Georgia until the age seventeen years was a very trying time. It was always very hot in the summer with long hazy days.

Children always heard the phrase, "It's better to be seen and not heard." I thought that to be poetic. There was much superstition in our culture. Many stories were told to me of times of old by Mom, aunts, and elderly people. Some people would talk of ghosts stories. Thereafter, I became afraid of the dark. That's also the time when we used "outhouses" for their waste. Long path from our backyard would lead to one. Mom told her children how to live in peace with your neighbor while loving God and others. Of course, everything started in our home. We were taught to have faith in God. Many of the schoolteachers (all colored), who taught all children, were good mentors too. I was surrounded by people with good moral, values, and strength despite all the hatred, bigotry, and segregation that I was born into. There and then was the way of life. I developed a mindset to be the best that I could be. I wanted more than what was around me. "Be" was inspired to write from that. At the age of ten, my brother (Jim) got us involved in going to the mass meetings for Civil Rights in my small town. That was first in 1960. I learned the freedom songs and how to make the placards (signs) to carry. We carried the signs where we did sit-ins and marches, demonstrations in protest to desegregate places against Negroes (black man). I took an oath of conduct to ready me for a peaceful marches. Me and my siblings, along with many young people, risks being arrested and endure long marches, carrying signs, beatings, and jail time. We were very active in the Civil Rights movement protests.

The Jim Crow system of laws were everywhere. The history making protest and demonstration March of 1963 to desegregate the

Martin Theater (only one in town) caused me to be arrested at the age of thirteen years old, July 11, 1963. Consequently, being jailed for forty-five days in a Georgia Stockade. That badge of honor was for standing up for my Civil Rights, which is my inalienable rights. Though it was for a great cause; the experience took away my innocence and left me traumatized.

For years afterward, I endured nightmares, earaches, and scars from the incarceration of that awful place. That is what inspired the poem "stockade." It cites the real horror surrounding the circumstances, also the poetry/poem, "What Is This I Dream Of?" The lasting struggle of the nightmares and night sweats plagued me for twenty-seven years. Frankly, we were socially unaccepted in every way and living as second-class citizens. The poem "Father, Dedicated to You" is written out not knowing him. My father died when I was only one year old. Because of my brothers who showed much love and support for me and my sisters, that poem was written for them in the family sense. "Mama Dearest" is definitely dedicated to Gertrude Lucille Johnson (mother). I love her and always will. She was dear to her sons and daughters.

This book of poetry/poems hopefully is for a family's heritage of values and spirituality, which is basically for everyone. "Sister, Sister" is for my sisters or anyone's sister, friend, young and old. Family is important to me. The poem "Shakespeare" is printed in the *International Book of Poets* through trial work. This book is written as to explain true feelings and the articulation of my childhood, Christian belief, adulthood, love, friendship, heritage, and personal experiences.

I pray that the reader, whether you are a teacher, professor, minister, school-age, mother, father, or regardless of gender, that you will find my book historically refreshing.

Poetry

Every time I write a poem
I feel that it should rhyme
As long as the words make sense (to me)
And placed from line to line.

Every time I write a poem,
It helps me speak a part.
Not all the time the line will rhyme
As long as it is from the heart.

Every time I write a poem,
The words flow from hand to pen.
I have to know what words to write,
Or the poem will never end.

Every time I write a poem,
It's hardly about you or me.
But if I continue to write this stuff,
A great poet I shall be.

Family

Be

I never resented sound truth
Where parents and teachers met
All the values and principles installed
In me, I won't ever forget.

"You can be anything
You want to be"
Was all I ever heard
No matter how tough
My classes seemed
That was my teachers'
Favorite word.

Often, Mom would say
In words so soft to me,
"My dear, darling girl, you
Can be whatever you want to be."

"Not only because in America
You can see what you want to see"
But what more importantly
In our democracy is
You can be what you choose to be.

Father, Dedicated to You

A father is a man, who
Loves his children so dear,
He becomes one with mother
Whom he truly does adore.

A father is strong and kind
He gives himself to all.
He makes his family feel safe
No matter what's the call.

A father has strong arms
That cradle you when you fall,
He has the patience of Job,
He shares the stubbornness of Paul.

Though I never knew my father
He passed when I was two,
He left my three brothers behind
My father, they are examples of you.

Mama Dearest

Ma was dear to all her children
She was all we had,
Ma was there through thick 'n' thin
Even when she was sad.

We always knew when trouble arrived
'Cause she would always pray,
She said, "God will Fix it, don't you worry,
He promised a Brighter Day."

Ma was dear to all her children
She taught us right from wrong
Ma gave us Love and fed us well
She wanted us to be strong.

Ma was dear to all her children
She was Blessed to me,
She showed Trust, mercy, and faith
And taught us INTEGRITY.

Memory of a Loved One

Life was given to us day by day
Our Love kept us special in every way
I'll remember your smile that shine so bright
I hear your laughter through the night
I'll hug your pillow.

God gave me joy that turn into peace
There was no great love under heaven beneath
The first time I saw your beautiful smile
I knew our love would last for a while.

But now there will be moments of sadness and grief
And many moments of sorrow
But only God can give relief.

I pray that you will rest for now
Until I meet you in heaven on High
Farewell, my love, for you'll forever be
Till Jesus call me home to be with thee.

Sister, Sister

Fate made us who we are
A choice we did not make
"Wasn't Mom's choice, neither was it Dad's,
But we are sisters for goodness' sake!"

Our eyes and smiles are so alike,
My hair is coarse and Light
Yours is soft, curly, and straight
That shapes a "face" to fit you right!

Sister, sister, you are my friend
Who shares secrets from year to year
Many in words and some in Laughter
My lovely sister, I hold you dear.

As time slips by us, sister,
I think I will let you know
Whatever made us sisters,
I love you and care even more.

Dedicated to Ada "Denise"

Thoughts

As the sand in an hourglass
So are the days of our lives.
As a secondhand sweeps the face of a clock
Seems to make the time pass
So are the days of our lives.

As the morning come up without the moon
So are the days of our lives.
As the sun shines away the overcast gloom
So are the days of our lives.

As the stars seem to twinkle in the sky
So are the days of our lives.

Birthday Wish

If I had three wishes
And each one came true
I know what I would wish for
Two will be for you

First I will wish for love
To show how much I care
In many hugs and kisses
Beautiful gifts from everywhere

Next I will wish for peace
And joy to follow your way
With laughter and friendship
On such a special day

Though the last one is simple
For everyone to see
It doesn't take three wishes
To say, "Happy Birthday" from me

Black Men Make the Difference

Listen up, brothers, you have your place
God made you wise and strong
You were formed in God's own image
It's time to separate right from wrong

Listen up, brother, seek first the kingdom
God will do the rest
You will have trials and tribulations
But in him you will be blessed

So stand up in your home and take control
Set an example of rules
Teach your sons and daughters to pray
And walk the little ones to school

You can be a big brother to boys in need
Please treat your wife as you should
Praise her efforts and show some respect
These things will do you some good

Work hard to have your own things in life
Educate you mind every day
Oh, what a great leader you'll become
When you just trust in God and pray

Really, you have come a long way here
So don't toss your talents aside
Wisely use your tools and build a new start
In the community where you abide

(Then God will bless and heal your people.)

Days of the Week

Sunday is the day to pray
Monday is the day to say,
"Tuesday will follow next in line"
Wednesday is halfway through the grind
Thursday is never the end
Friday is when my pay begin
Saturday is the last of the week
Rest and pleasure, I shall seek.

Breathless

Early in the morning,
As I arose in pure serenity,
The cool dew was crisp
And shiny in a glassy frost.

Your sweet breath must have
Blown across the earth's
Sweet sleeping breast...

The magnificent frost
On the grass and leaves,
Covering the birds' nests
In the tallest trees.

Everything around me
Was evident of your
Sweet breath
That covered the ground.

Even the wild animals tracks
Revealed your omnipresence.
The sight of it all found me
In "awe" of your greatness!
And left me breathless.

The Earth

The earth is full of colors
different reds, browns, and blues
Then there are people of various skin tones
And vehicles of assorted hues

Some buildings are painted with yellow
The grass is the color of green
The rocks and stones are gray and white
A pretty sight to be seen

All the oceans are blues and wide
The waters are deep and cold
Larges white vessels sail the mighty tides
On earth from times of old

Some of the sand is brown or white
Some of the soil is black
Some of the dirt is red with chalk

The leaves are different colors in Autumn
Bright oranges, reds, and greens
Oh, what an earth of beautiful colors
Especially the flowers in the spring

Animals too have various colors
Some large and short with hair
Their coats comes in all sizes
We're all earthlings in God's care

Free Spirit

Oh my! Oh how!
I wish I could fly.
To touch treetops
Near the sky.

To see the earth
From up above
And drop sweet kisses
And spread some love.

To soar like an eagle
Over mountains high,
Oh my! Oh how!
I wish I could fly!

If I Had My Way

If I had my way
Today, I would say
Peace and Freedom
Comes what may

If I sang a song
About love
I would thank
My God above

If I call anyone
To talk
I would say
Let us talk a walk

I f I had my way today
I will say, "Be good and be kind"
So this will bring
Us peace of mind.

I

I lie on the soft green grass
Looking up to the blue sky
At different shapes of clouds
Floating above very high

I tried to imagine being
A large bird or airplane
Up, up, up way above
The ground where I lay
On a lazy, hazy summer day

Imagine

What will a tree be like
If it didn't have its leaves,
Would it be like having legs
That didn't have the knees?

What would an ocean be like
If it didn't have its fish,
Perhaps like eating a bowl of soup
Without a spoon or dish?

What good would a song be
If it didn't have a melody,
Perhaps like a locked door
That didn't have a proper key?

What good will a set of wings serve
If they didn't have a back to hug,
Perhaps like lying on a cold hard floor
Without a comfortable rug?

What good will a face be
If it didn't have the eyes,
Perhaps like giving the foolish ones
All knowledge instead of the wise?

Shadow

I think that I should never see
My shadow walks in front of me
On such a cloudy day
Nothing following after me

When the sky is blue
And the rain is gone
Over the path
I'd trod alone

I'll wait for the sun
To brighten my day
I'll have my shadow
To follow me today

Shakespeare

Shakespeare was a great playwright
A poet, novelist, and more,
Theatrical plays, movies, and poems
Came from his work for sure.

Plays like *Romeo and Juliet*
Are favorites for all times,
Romantic songs and hamlet plays
Words remembered from line to line.

Shakespeare's work was mystical
He was sometimes critical,
Plays and poems of love he wrote,
It seems Othello was pitiful.

Shakespeare was great for his mind
A visionary from the start,
The odes, the writings from his time
Still lingers in our heart.

Shakespeare, O great Shakespeare,
God must have so favor in you
For you believed in mankind
Leaving a motto, "To thyself be true."

Smile

I think I'll grin
Oh no!
Maybe, I will smile
But only for a little while
Oh well!
Perhaps, I'll laugh
Out loud!
Who will see my smile?
Who will hear my laugh?
Who will know
Why I feel this
Giggle wants to grow?

Springtime

Sitting at the window
Looking in a stare
At all the beautiful birds
Soaring through the air

As I ponder in my thoughts
Scanning the lilies field,
And all the wild flowers bloom
Just beyond the hill.

I can see the water pond
The butterflies and bees
The romping little baby fawn
Tree leaves swaying in the breeze

Way up in the blue sky
The sun shines so bright,
I'm just staring out my window
Before daylight turns to night.

Symbolic of…

If I had an orchard,
I'd plan every tree there be.
It would look like a garden
For everyone to see.

There will be many colors,
The trees stand tall in a row.
Many bright leaves that shade the ground
Sowing good fruit as the harvest grow.

Some will be like beautiful flowers,
Each will be a symbol of love
Growing to share as "ours."

The orchard really is just a metaphor for life.
This is a sense of unity if we want beauty for all instead of strife!

Words

Words are a way of expression
Whether they be kind or sad
Words can be comforting
Helpful or sound silly
And glad.

Words can filter anger
Can stir wrath and shame
"Words can fly," some may say
If used as the wrong name.

Words make great sentences
Can ask questions too.
Words give many meanings
To help teach me and you.

Words can be beautiful
If spoken in a prayer
We need words to communicate
In the world that we all share.

Spiritual

Angels

Angels are in many forms
Many forces that are unseen
Angels are encamped around us
Standing guard as kings or queens

Angels, they say, all have wings
Some may be big or small
Angels come in various colors
Some are even short or tall.

Angels are sent to protect us
Even when we are bad
Angels have the power to save us
When times are happy and sad.

Angels are heavenly creatures
Sent to do an earthly chore
Angels are made to join us
Until God call his children ashore.

Easter

Easter is here
Easter is there
Easter must be everywhere!

All over the world
Celebrated by boys and girls.

Faith

Faith is like a farmer
Who plants his seeds so deep,
Faith is hoping the sun and rain
Will bring a Harvest to reap.

Faith brings another day to him
He's up at the crack of dawn,
Planting more seeds to Harvest
Before the morning sun.

Faith is like the midnight
That reaches for the morn,
Faith is liken to a Rooster
Which crows before the dawn.

Faith is like a full moon
That brightens the darkest night,
Faith is the substance of things hoped for
That will guide us to the Light.

Hope

Hope is like a flowing river
That goes from sea to sea,
Hope is like a love song
That stirreth up inside of me.

Hope is like a Ray of Sun
That caseth forth its light!
Hope is waiting for the moment
That changes wrong to Right.

Hope is that thing with faith
That seems to brighten the way,
Hope turns sad times into Joy
And makes hope for another day!

I'm Free

Like magic in my life,
Your spirit has rule me.
If the words of prayer that worked,
Surely you have set me free.

As Life is set for Liberty
Grace has sustained my Path,
O glory be to the Holy King
Thy Promises and Love we hath.

Thy Breath is sweet on my face
But let me mourn my sin,
My Spiritual guide who ruleth me
Will endureth to the end.

I'm free, I'm free, I'm free
As a bird in the top of a tree
God has rescued me, you see!
I'm free, indeed, I'm free.

My Plea

Clouds floating freely
The bursts of rain and dew
Envelopes their shapes.

Make ready my heart
To receive thy word
Gird my mind
To be fixed on your Divine.

Perfect peace passes
With much understanding
In this earthly vessel
That carries my condemning

You bared the cross
The bloodstained banner
For me and all
Who are sinners

No way I can look up
And live
Without your life
That you give

I lift my heart up
I bow it before thee
Keep me in your word
Lord divine, accept my plea.

Oh, how glorious is thy name
The sun rises herself high in the sky
Bright with the clear big universe
Ever so high puffs of distance

Later the enchantment of twinkling
Stars light up the darkness of the sky's path
Quietly the moon smiles slyly
To assist other heavenly bodies
Beyond my grasps
What glorious mystery to behold.

Poem for a Small Child

Precious, precious, little one
How did you come to be?
You must be a gift from God
He sent you here to me.

I will give you a name of a flower
Or perhaps the name of a tree
I can call you beautiful
It is all left up to me.

Precious, precious, little one
To me, you are so dear
You are my gift from God above,
To love and hold you near.

You are a blessing to me!

Success

Go back to your foundation
God is standing by,
Where it's an unseen power
Perhaps we don't understand why.

The landmark is where it all begin
Be positive, work hard to your best.
No matter where you came form
You're going to have trials and some tests.

Obey the Great Commandments
They are known by the "ten,"
To love God first and your fellow man
Is where your success begin.

Oh, come and taste the Lord
Just try this simple way
It's easy if you just trust him
Your eternity awaits at Judgment Day.

The Bible

B is of Basic
I is for Instructions
B is for Before
L is for Leaving
E is for Earth

Our Greatest Book
What is mankind? Who is the Creator?
Or do we need to know?
I am complete in my spirit
I am complete in myself
But who am I really?

Are there others like me?
Do they feel what I feel?
The man that I see looks the same
Why are there so many of us?

We had different purposes, some of us
Have that same talents or interests
Why? What need to have so many
That perhaps sang the same songs.

Why are we different colors
Why not all the same race.
Confusion will really set in
What do you mean?

Is evil the greater force
For mankind? Hope not!

My Soul

Where is my strength?
Is it deep in my soul
Where is my courage?
Does it come before a fight
What is my humility
Is it after an embarrassing moment?

What is honesty?
Is it the same as being true
What makes me laugh?
Is it how I perceive a joke?

What is obedience?
Does it mean to do what I'm told
From deep in the heart
It starts deep in the soul

Down in My Soul

Whew! Sit down and take a breath
You're been running too long
But time is moving so fast
It seems just a matter of time

My mind is free, and so is the soul
Daily I'm spinning fast into the future
Presently I'm pleased just to know
My spirit take control beyond my grasp

I feel a force that challenge my mind
To write my thoughts down, I desire
It's reality that bites at me
My faith and hope pulls me through.

The Word

In the beginning was the Word
It came to set us free,
There was darkness all around us
It brought light to you and me.

The Word came forth with a shout
Its powerful sound did reigned
The gift of God began to rule
The earth began its form.

It gave the sun to rule by day
The moon to rule by night
And all the heavenly stars where made
Soon gave the earth its light.

Great is the kingdom of our Lord
He made us in his image,
The Word was God from the start
The author of our faith and finisher!

Forever

Like the smell of a soft, fine perfume
That lingers through the air
Your spirit is everlasting
You taught me well and fair.

As precious as the memories are,
Your love and faith was there
I shall soon come to meet thee
O Great Emanuel, O Emanuel

So persistent as the morning sun
That comes to light the way
You sustained me and stay amid us
A blessing of every day.

The integrity and morals I learned
During the years of hope with stride,
You taught me well and because of that
Yes, I'm black and very proud.

Friend

When one is in need of help
You seem to be right there
No matter how hard it seems
You're the one that care.

You laid your life down for me
So that I can believe and live
The whole foundation is only you
A friend can only give

When woes and sorrows come my way
I know whom I can trust
The love you gave, my faith in you
Was given to all of us

My love for you, my faith and hope
Will last till the end
Thanks! There is no doubt
You are my one true friend!

Love Is

As a melody to a song
Thy love is sweet to me
As sounds of many waters
The rivers all run free

As the sun rising in the sky
The birds will sing to the morn.
As the gentle air breezes
As the sound of a french horn

As a stroke of a painter's brush
Will soon needs a picture frame
But can never capture the wailing
Sound of a distant train.

As a candle that lights the dark
Can cast awkward shadows away
As the little rudder on a large ship
That guides it thru a bay.

My Valentine

My valentine, oh, heart of mine
Sweet roses at your feet
My joy, my love so divine
A lovely sonnet to greet

Be my valentine forever, dear
Like great wine so sweet
Cupid sent thy love to me
Makes my heart skips a beat

Truly you belong to me now
You must know it too
Oh, heart of mine, my valentine
Sincerely, I love you, true

Struttin' Right Up

Old sassy colored girl
With your skin so fair.
And your red ruby lips
Has a luscious flare.

Your large round eyes
With a piercing glare.
Your chocolate brown legs
Struttin' here 'n' there.

Hey, face the facts, sister,
With your full figure bod.
It's very sensuous and sassy
Makes many heads nod.

Your honey-dipped chocolate
Your brown-bronze glow
Old sassy colored girl
You got it going on, you know!

When'er I see you, it's like love at first sight.
When'er I'm near you, my heart skips a beat.
Oh, tell me now, tell me, my love.
Whisper in my ear words that sweep me off my feet.

You've got a style of your own
That comes so naturally,
So add that Love, Joy, and Liberty.

Black History

Africa

Africa, you are the mother country
With your land of beauty so fair
You are great in riches and precious things
That's why the garden of Eden is there.

Africa, you have many birds of prey,
The elephants, lions, and tigers
The hot summer sun that warms the air
Invites your animals to the Niger.

Africa, you are rich with wealth
Because of your precious stones
Your oil and other fine quality gems
Oh, what a pity violence that skins flesh to bones.

Africa, please help your people see
How sinful some of them have become,
Just centuries ago, man was placed
On earth in you the earthly home.

Africa, all your natives have been
Scattered throughout your land
They are divided into opposing sides
Leaving your heritage and language fading away
And is placed in some other's hand.

Africa, look to the Creator now
For he wants to heal your land
From your beautiful garden of Eden
Is where the Master's plan began.

Discrimination Among Coloreds/Blacks (The Shade of Skin Tone)

Help me, my sisters and brothers
We all are keepers of one another
God made us, our shapes and sizes
Light, black, chocolate, and brown.

There is no time for envy nor strife
Everyone has got to be nice
Brown skin, coco, and dark
Almost white, lighter than black
Was not anyone's choice.

Let us put aside pride and jealousy.
We all are one flesh and created to be free.

It is God that matters, you know.
The more we care, our spirits will show,
There shouldn't be hatred, jealousy nor malice
The burden cross of love is ours to carry.

Justice Let It Stand

Justice let it stand
Like a wildfire
From country to country
Should be a man's desire

Let it roll down
In every town and valley
Let it be shown on
Street, lane, and alley

Let it wipe out
Every unkind act
Putting love firstly
To make an impact

Let it roll down
Like a river or stream
Remembering that speech
Of Dr. King's "I Have a Dream"

Martin L. King and Elvis, the "King" of Rock

What a memory! What a memory!
Could it be that bad?
Some may say it's history
Others may call it "sad."
It's about these two great people,
Where one's life begin,
And about the other one
Whose life came to a tragic end.
In the city named "Memphis,"
These two called Elvis and Martin.
One was titled "king," and one was named King.
These two people are not forgotten.
In the month of April each year
Elvis and Martin are celebrated.
This one we can all understand,
So long lived the "kings" in history.

We all share respect and dedicate it to
Those who left their lasting music
And liberty to all in the land.

Once Upon a Time

Once upon a time
In the hometown of mine
During the early sixties
Was hatred, bigotry,
And crime

The law said:
Colors were black
And white people
Governed by Jim Crow laws
All separated by train tracks
Without any real cause

There was tension in the air
Separation and segregationists
Were every where
Through signs of despair
Sadness and gloom
New hope and bright future
Was about to bloom.

Stand For What You Believe

S is for Stand
T is for Tall
A is for And
N is for Never
D is for Depart

F is for For
O is for Often
R is for Rich

W is for Word
H is for Heart
A is for All
T is for Teach

Y is for You
O is for Our
U is for Us

B is for Blessed
E is for Everlasting
L is for Love
I is for I
E is for Every
V is for Victory
E is for Eternal

Southern Memories

Move On

Tis' ain't no time for laffin'
So change da silly smirk
Ain't no need ta sit down
Cuz standin' didn't work.

Put your hearts together now
Ya know what you've been tole
Show some respect for the elderly,
Our colored folk of ole.

Y'all are used ta wearin' them britches
Who you trying ta fool.
So put down them guns
And hurry back ta school.

Remember where you came from
Tis ain't been dat long
So clean up your act, child
And get a brand-new song.

Respect yourself first
Or ain't nobody else will.
Put down them dar drugs
And give da streets a chill.

So set yourself a goal, now
Tis ain't no time to waste.
Come on sustas, come on, brothas,
Let us all make haste.

Pó Man

Po' man from down yonder
They say you don't fit in.
Yore clothes iz tattered rags
Does it mean ya done sin?

Tis' like a curse, on you
Seems like ain't no hope.
Yore po' English usage
Makes ya sound like a dope

Hard times came yore way
More times than not.
Po' man self-esteem is gone
But hope is all ya got.

Ain't nobody here to
Look out fa' ya'.
Guess you gotta look
Out fa yourself.

Dem dar tattered ole clothes
Don't say much for anyone.
Hold your head up high and
See what you have done!

Ya came from great kings
Po' man, this ya should know.
Whether ya from way down yonder
Or from the state of OHIO.

T'ain't no lazy gals here no mo'
They all went dancin' down the row.

Childhood Memories

Barefoot

Barefoot black children
Playing in the sun
Screaming loudly,
Jumping, laughing,
And having fun.

Tattered shirts, tattered shorts
Just about the knees
Ripping, running,
Playing stickball, four
Little boys in dirty tees

Girls playing hopscotch
Singing and jumping rope
In tattered dresses
With big sashes
Playing the game of "hope"

Barefoot all day
But not in the park
Playing on red dirt roads
Before it got too dark

Children

Children, children
(In) Sizes short and tall.
Famous children, not so
Famous children, they are one in all.

Little children, big children
Sad children, mad children.
Happy children, glad children,
Good children and bad.

Colored children, brown children
Red children, black children
Stout children, fat children
Skinny children, and white (Caucasian).

They (all) are children of God.
They too are special people.
The precious little gifts to behold
Children are wonderful little creatures.

Children will be children.

My Town

There is the rural town
So deep in the South
Vestiges of slavery and segregation
Still lingers about.

The small shanty houses
On the plantation still stand
With long rows of cotton
On many acres of land

There's hatred and separation
Visibly seen in despair
And the rebel's confederate flag
Still hanging everywhere

"Hey, boy!" is still shouted at the
Old men of color
It doesn't matter
If it's a father, son, or a brother

What would Martin say
If he was yet alive?
He would encourage his dream
So the people could survive!

Hometown of Americus, Georgia, (1950–1960)

Summertime

'Tis the lazy, hazy days
Of summertime
Recalls the memories of
The childhood of mine

Softball, dodgeball, stickball,
And jump rope
When playing as a black child,
Praying for our hope

Deep in the South
Hot in the sun
Running on the red dirt,
Laughing and having fun

Little Sally Walker
Sitting in a saucer
Weeping and wishing
About what you have done.

Leesburg Memories

When children were seen
Playing in the sun
They were skipping, running,
And having fun

When children were happy
And trying to be good
They would chase each other
Down in the woods

When children came home
After walking from school
They had to remember
The Golden Rule

There were many chores
And homework to do
First, they'd change their clothes
Their socks and shoes too

Americus, Georgia in '63

Americus, Georgia in '63
There were obvious signs of bigotry
Laws of segregation were everywhere
White supremacist groups did not care

The hatred they had for people of colors
Was blatant and vicious
Toward my sisters and brothers

There were perpetrators, spectators,
Instigators and violators,
Vigilantes, agitators, KKKs,
And negro haters

We marched with our placards
And sang the freedom songs
We were beaten and jailed
While making history at home

Many fought for their freedom
To change the Jim Crow laws
Now Americus has signs of liberty
And no more segregated walls

Thirteen Is Ten plus Three

At thirteen, I wanted to be free
The change had to begin with me,
So I marched in a group formed
By SNCC—"Snick."

I did not know my fate
But I had to repeat,
The demonstrations meet
Only three times a week.

As the time went past,
I had to join the protest at last,
On my way during the demonstration,
That day, I was beaten and dragged
Labeled and tagged as a "freedom fighter's" way.

At thirteen, I was arrested and taken
To a place that was cold, vacant,
Abandoned and old, there
My story began but was never told.

I was locked in with thirty-one others
All thirteen-year-old sisters and no brothers.
Though I was kept alive
Through prayer I had to survive,
That horrible "stockade" dive.

Misery

When strong wind blows
Leaves fall from the tree
Like unto a metaphor of life
That causes "misery"

With trials and temptations
That come my way
Shattering my comfort
On any given day

Sometimes I may give in
And soon prepare,
When these winds approach
Me, I am aware

I can stand strong and
Be like the tree
Without the fallen leaf
Caused by misery!

Memories of the Stockade

Oh, wretched place of fear, so cold I found
It taught me about hope and peace abound
Faith gave me a prayer, and that brought me strength
Although they joy renewed my mind.

Oh, I thought of times when I cried
Oh, help me for you are my guide,
Then peace came so deep within
And I would sing and smile again.

Away from my home, you place me there
Perhaps not realizing how much you care
It took some time for me to see, but I know that now
Your precious love was always near.

Days and years had passed since then
But it's wisdom you give and grace you send,
And it's you who made the change in me
Regardless of my part in America's history.

There was pain and suffering…

Traumatized

I sat behind the bars
In a small town's jail cell
Hoping for justice and
Righteousness to prevail.

I was accuse of a crime
Without due process of the law
The stockade forty-five days incarceration
Was one great big flaw.

I dined on raw burgers that wasn't
Fit to eat, I didn't get fat,
Made me so sick, and weak.

After two weeks in, I was given a tin cup
As I reached for warm water
Under the shower head up
I had scrapes and bruises
From lying on the cold floor.
No bed, no blankets, no mattress, no fun
No toilet, no bath, only bars, no door.

I was there for four weeks without proper care
Inhuman treatments I had to share.
I was taken in a paddy wagon, the same way out
If it wasn't for the pictures, I would have died, no doubt.

Memories of the forty-five days in the Leesburg, Georgia, Stockade at twelve years old in 1963.

Black Night

The pitch-black nights were
Humid and long
Listening to all kinds of
Creatures chanting their songs

The sounds of crickets, frogs,
Dogs, and night owls
Sending messages to nightlife
Prowlers

Oh, the summer sleepless night
Where the moths fly
Around the old porch light

Mosquitoes sang, lightning bugs
Fly, night crawlers creep
And bats fly blindly in the
Black night sky

Squatting mosquitoes after dark
Is common on a hot summer
Dark night, too humid to sleep.
Feeling sweaty and gritty

Sheer blackness all around me
Scary ghostly sounds swishing
Through my mind

Nightmares

After My Release from the Stockade

What does it means when I dream of thee?
You were from long ago
The changes and times have changed me now
The wounds are fresh "No mo'."

What does it mean when I dream of thee?
You're a struggle from my past
The suffering that I once endured
Old memories only last.

What does mean when I dream of thee?
Your place wreaked of hate and grief
The stench of fear couldn't break me none
'Cause hope brought some relief.

Someday I pray I will understand
What this dream had meant to me
My fate or destiny before eternity
Has no meaning of this dream about thee.

Reminiscence
(Incarceration: 1965 Civil Rights)

The sultry summer night
Way out rural
The quiet pitch black
Still darkness. I lie on this
Cold hard concrete floor
Shut up from my family
A world away, yet not
So distant. Though other
Little girls are here.

My participation in a "cause"
To change a system
That created hatred,
Separation, and condemnation
My heart and my mind
Grieved to be at home
Wrapped in my mother's arm
To be bathed and fed
While needing and wishing
For my own bed

The real memory of the plight
Was all forty-five days indeed
This I was chosen for...
Did not make a movie star
Though I feel blessed
When I reminisce of my
UNEXPLAINABLE TEST
I look not back...with regret
Just a ponder of my life
That helped change things
For the rest.

Transition

When one is young, life is carefree.
What do the youth care?
The expression to live and life…
Is felt and seen without despair.

Adolescence is a growing spirit without
Rules, regrets or plans.
A time of irresponsibility of self
Chasing the winds without demands.

Adulthood comes quickly for sure
Teachings and experiencing life
"If you'd known what you know now,
Perhaps you would have waited
To be that husband or wife."

Old age is a blessing that
Should come with much wisdom.
It's been said, "Twenty-twenty is hindsight."
Life teaches us all a lesson.

About the Author

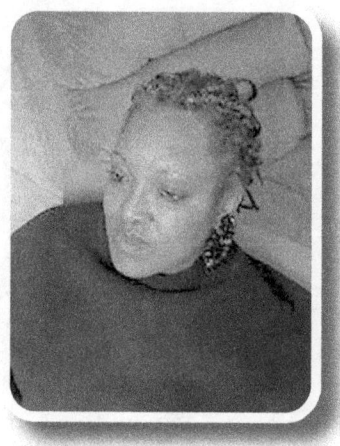

Lulu Westbrook Griffin, now fifty years later, lives outside of Rochester, New York. An agent of change, educator, poet, an author, and writer. She has won many awards, certificates, a proclaimation day, the keys to the city of Niagara Falls / Buffalo, New York, local freedom awards, heroes award, and many more, including the 2007 Dr. Martin Luther King Jr. "I Have a Dream Award. Also, her story was written up in the *Essence Magazine* in 2006, "The Stolen Girls of Leesburg, Georgia: A Civil Rights Story 1963." These poems/poetry speaks of history in Americus, Georgia, part of a historical revolution. Lulu's story was first shared in her local newspaper, the *Democrat and Chronicles*, Rochester, New York in 1997.

Printed in the USA
CPSIA information can be obtained
at www.ICGtesting.com
LVHW050527170224
772066LV00002B/571